As I Was Saying

MARION FRAZER

CALEDON PUBLIC LIBRARY 01

 FriesenPress

Suite 300 - 990 Fort St
Victoria, BC, V8V 3K2
Canada

www.friesenpress.com

Copyright © 2019 by Marion F. Frazer
First Edition — 2019

All rights reserved.

No part of this publication may be reproduced in any form, or by any means, electronic or mechanical, including photocopying, recording, or any information browsing, storage, or retrieval system, without permission in writing from FriesenPress.

ISBN
978-1-5255-3991-6 (Hardcover)
978-1-5255-3992-3 (Paperback)
978-1-5255-3993-0 (eBook)

1. Poetry, Canadian

Distributed to the trade by The Ingram Book Company

Table of Contents

Write Me a Poem 1

All in the family... 3
After the Funeral 5
I've Never Been Able 6
Letter to Nancy 7
Marion and Judy 10
The Mind Must Have a Nose 13
My Grandmother's Hands 14
Walls Become Windows 17
Wrestling in the Dark 19

As for politics... 21
Being Political 23
Revolution 24
You Wonder 25

Being a parent... 27
Being a parent 29
Four 30
Jack & Frosty 31
I was Yours 34
Mother's Day 36
Six 37

Dealing with destiny... 39
Aging 41
Dealing with Destiny 43
Funny 44
I Thought I Knew 45
Lately, 46
Remember 47
Stained Glass 48

From different angles... 51
December 53
Diana 55
Empty Rooms 56
The Floors 59
Forsythia 61
L'entranger 62
Trees 63
You Can't Write 65

Growing up Canadian... 67
About Winter 69
Scents of Summer 70
Summer in Saskatchewan 71
Swords, Knives and Daggers 72

Having a dog... 73
Dogs 75
Balker and the Babe 76

Only Human... 77
Antiques 79
Bath Water 80
Getting Colours Done 82
Guilt 83
Martha 85
Photograph 86
Procrastination 87
You Know, 89

Things that go bump in the night... 91
Ghost 93
The House on Elm Tree Lane 96
Stalker 99

Women, men, and sometimes, love... 101
After Dark 103
The First Moment of Love 105
Growing Fonder 107
When He Looked at Me 109
Without You 110
Watching You 111
Women and Men 112
Acknowledgements 115

To family and friends,
and to
the light
within

Write Me a Poem

he said
and I said
I'd love to
but that isn't
how
it works

poetry
wakes you up
at night
or
grabs your mind
in the
daytime
and shakes your
imagination
until

you forget about
sleep
or work
in the struggle to wind
the twisting words
into a shape
you hope
will bind them
with meaning

All in the family...

After the Funeral

You ask me
if I'll be coming back
some day
and your eyes
ask
if the pain will
be too much.

Don't worry.
Both my parents
are buried on this island
and I'll be back
to visit
the crevice
in my heart
they used
to fill.

I've Never Been Able

to write a poem
for my mother

It's like trying to describe a war
you fought in,
or
the sound of your baby
dying

All I can say is
every cell, every breath
of me
is
because she was my mother,
and I will feel
her voice
in my sleep and waking
all my life.

Letter to Nancy

Dear
little cousin,
when you came
to us
with your
tiny arms
and legs
(at fifteen, I could
circle your
two-year-old thigh
with my finger and thumb)
we wondered
how anything
so small
and perfect
could be alive

We didn't
know
what we were doing
to you
when we gave you
that new
name
of ours

For us
you were instantly
part of the family;
we never dreamed
how for so many
long years,
it wasn't
like that
for you,
how long
you looked
into the darkness
until your eyes
ached,
trying to see
the face
of your first mother

So blind
we were;
we never realized
your need
to melt yourself
into the warm gold
of lovely faces
like yours,
to bind yourself
into black braids,
rejecting
our fair hair
and pale
skins

Then
that night
when my aunt was dying,
you knew then,
didn't you,
where to find
your mother?

She'd loved you
so much
so long
she never thought
she needed to go looking for you
in the darkness
until
you found her.

Marion and Judy

That summer
Skinny, Nordic-tan-blond boy/girl
I tried to keep up
as we ran across the prairie
cutting our feet
on the burnt-dry stubble
hiding under bushes
picking berries
envying our brothers
with their twig bows and arrows
because they got to shoot
at gophers
teasing your little sister
being obnoxious

Cousin
you were as close as I ever got
to a sister
that summer

Now
I'm still running to
keep up

You grew up so much faster
than I did

Married before me
I can still see you
on your wedding day
the calmest one in the house
so quiet, radiant
and certain

We danced all night

You were the one
with the clutch full of children
happy, busy wife
and mom

You were the one
who first knew heartbreak
nursing your Joe
through agonizing months

But honey
whatever could prepare you
for this?

I don't know

To lose your man
and now
your boy

All I can say is
you're beating
me again

to heaven.

The Mind Must Have a Nose

The mind must have a nose
because
today I can smell my grandparents' house

Earth, oil, sweat:
garage

Mold, damp, dust, bottled sweetness:
cellar

Wet raincoats, hot days, coconut, stale cookies:
mud room

Cedar, lavender, bleach, ironed sheets:
bedroom

Christmas
never completely over, even in July:
spruce
and
secrets

You know
that house has been gone
thirty years?

My Grandmother's Hands

were always busy

healing...
She was a nurse through war and peace.

Her lightning fingers saved my life once,
as, caught in a wringer,
my long hair was spinning
my scalp from my head.
She was almost eighty then
but still carried surgical scissors
at her belt.

And I remember
how there'd be pounding on the cottage door
at all hours;
Gran, in her seventies, first call
to pull another life
from Our Lake.

nurturing...
She had plenty of practice.

The eldest girl of nine,
naturally she brought up the six younger ones;
she was to be the pillar of her mother's age
until
her eldest brother helped her
to escape
to nursing school
(she wanted to be a doctor)
and then my Gramp.

Gramp,
four children, twelve grandchildren
and the great-grandchildren too
(she always wanted to fly a plane)
reaped the benefit
of her experience.

nourishing...
I still feel tired to think
of all the meals
three times a day
(not counting snacks and special stuff)
she made
for family, friends, socials,
and threshing crews,
then, finally,
for herself.

No dishwashers then!

creating...
Never still.
Those clever hands
tore apart sweaters
in the Thirties
to knit them up again,
dove-tailed fine cabinets
in the Fifties
for fun.
She taught herself to weave
and crochet
anything to dress the home and family,
satisfying her gnawing urge
to make.

No wonder
it broke my mother's heart
to see those fingers
crippled, gnarled, and arthritic
in her nineties
dancing in her lap
as
she twirled her thumbs.

Walls Become Windows

She
was ninety-two
when I finally met her

We'd been
having tea
(We'd been having tea together
since I could hold a cup,
almost.
She loved to tell a story
of a sleepy three-year-old me
demanding tea at midnight
"to cheer me up")

But that day
she was frightened.
(She who'd always been
all saucy fearlessness)
Her fragile independence
would be sacrificed
to her age

Age had never mattered to her
before
(She was the one who'd
left the seniors' home
bored ministering to the need of
"seniors" younger than
herself)

So
I heard her real voice.
(Not the one that had sung me
through journeys,
as I snuggled, nestled
into her soft-in-all-the-right-places
body)

Extraordinary
how those familiar wrinkles,
like the name loved so long,
were just the fabric of a wall with many
pictures
on it

That day
when the wall became a window
lucky,
I was there.

Wrestling in the Dark

against
the devils
in his mind

Morning dawns grey
greyness shadows
every day

Writhing convolutions
of his mind
snatch at glimmering
sunbeams
in moments
of mine

but I can beat him
my weapons
lie in my life
grow from my grief
for him

As for politics…

Being Political

Is a matter of wanting
isn't it,
wanting to lead society,
an orderly animal,
by a different coloured chain?

What's your colour?

Revolution

just never seems to work out properly,
does it?

Ragged, starving, you pull on
your red stocking cap
with the tricolour cockade
hoping to achieve a baguette a day,
then
aghast
clutch at doorways
as you're swept away
in the torrent of blood
pouring out of those
red caps.

No use to say
you didn't really
mean it.

You gaze in horror at the
devastation
spiraling from your
intentions
and realize you can't
unerupt
a volcano.

You Wonder

how we could be so stupid
as to believe
we're making things
better
by exchanging
parcels of food
to last
one family one day
for the privilege of destruction with impunity

But then
when you look at us
sitting, eyes glazed
with incomprehension
conferred
by clean underwear
every day
ever-running water
and
pop and chips

you understand.

Being a parent...

Being a parent

you greet
with astonishment
the knowledge
not only that you would give
your life
for that life
but that your greatest fear
is that
you may be prevented
from making
the trade.

Four

Right now
We're taking a break
From "No!"Through the fingers
Stuffed in your mouth
You are singing.

Right now
The caretaker of your dreams,
I hold them in my hands,
Delicate
As dandelion seeds
Sparkling
In the sun.

Right now
A tuft of silky hair
Tickles the side of my nose;
Your knee
Is
Firmly planted in my stomach,
As the fingers
Not in your mouth
Scamper
Up and down my cheek
Exploring
The infinite dimensions
Of the room in my heart
Called
William.

Jack & Frosty

Will
has
two stuffed snowmen
on his bed
together
they're a lesson
in
love.

We bought Jack
one day
in a panic of almost losing
Frosty
(better to have a replacement
handy
we thought).

He sits there
fat and immaculate
his white plush
silky
his hat firm
and straight
his carrot nose
perfect in its
dimensions
his eyes
shiny black stones
his mouth
five black marbles
a toy.

Frosty
slumps on Will's
pillow
thin, grubby, plush worn off
in places
especially 'round the neck
where we had to quickly
sew him up
his faded old hat laps limply
over dull black eyes
his carrot nose
is battered
(he's probably been flying again).

But
even I find
he feels comforting
to cuddle
(you'd swear he cuddles back)
those two black eyes
shine
with the comic sadness
of a clown.

No doubt about it
love is painful
but
ready or not
does magically
awaken
life.

I was Yours

from the first
cry.

You lay
swaddled in a blue blanket
a white cotton cap
jammed on your head
like a candle extinguisher
your brow furrowed
your misty blue eyes
squinting
against the light.

It was
a full five minutes
before I saw you
and caught the
intensity
of that frown;
even then
you needed to
figure things out.

Still
the only sound
you could make
was as individual
as your tiny
fingerprint;
I could pick out
that sound
from twenty others
strong, urgent, demanding
deep.

I guess
I knew right away
how it would be—
you were yourself
and I was
yours.

Mother's Day

Newspaper photographs
are a source of terror
for mothers.

You see the faces
staring out at
you
over their tragic
little stories
and pray that chance
will deliver
your own desperately
beloved faces
from
Evil.

Six

Cuddling
is becoming endangered
lately;
each public kiss
precious,
snatched
from time,
sweet,
but conscious,
looking over its
shoulder,
wondering how long
before the first one
is wiped off.
M-O-O-M!

Now,
when my
getting-so-big-isn't-he-he'll-be tall
son
fills my lap,
accepts,
or even asks for
a snuggle,
the shock of
baby softness
as his cheek
touches mine,
or
I sneak
a kiss,
holds
our first moments
together
with the
anticipation
of
empty
arms.

Dealing with destiny...

Aging

Wondering what kind of old woman
I'll be
seems a matter of
geography and clichés
at the moment.

Will I be old from
Montreal or Manhattan:
sharp-eyed, spare, chic, knowing,
sophisticated, slim-gone-to-skin,
getting around in sleek black suits
to symphonies
and openings
in cabs?

Or old from
the Midwest:
perpetually baking,
my body a pillow,
a cozy country for
grandchildren
to settle in?

Or will I be
old from the West Coast:
in caftans, my long hair
loose, or coming out of
a bun,
up on natural medicines, into crafts,
eccentric,
drying my own herbs,
wishing I was
Native?

Hoping I won't be
Bowery-old:
vacant eyed, lost
in two or three coats,
a dirty felt hat
jammed on my head,
begging,
as I snarl abuse
at passers-by
between ramblings.

But it's more curiosity
than fear
at the moment.

Dealing with Destiny

High
Above your head
Muted sunlight filters
Through murky water

You watch
Silver bubbles of breath race upwards
As dreamily
You glance down
At your particular weeds
Weaving your feet
Into half-buried black branches

Life is a choice now
Dark ribbons float in your mouth
Tangle in your hair
Will you reach down
Ever so slowly
To release yourself from this bondage
Burst up
Exploding lost light into brilliant fragments
Gasp fresh sweet cold air
Or
Curl softly into the warm bed
Of dreams?

Funny

isn't it
how a person can get
used to
anything—

a sliver, a limp,
a missing limb,
the screaming silence
of Will's room
with Will not in it…

I'm getting used now
to the distant, brittle sound
of
my own laughter,
just as
they must have gotten used
to
the leper's bell.

I Thought I Knew

heartache—
the weight of black stone
in the chest
throbbing the body
is familiar.

But this
I want a wolf's claws
to tear it out.

Is this
what they mean
by
bleeding internally?

Lately,

I seem to be getting slower
at everything
slower to dress, slower to finish
thinking slow,
it's always
half an hour later
than I thought it was.

Aging, then,
must be
like a Newfoundland harbour
where you watch
the ice flows
day after day,
sailing together, sailing...
'til you wake up
one morning
still
surprised
to see
freeze up.

Remember

that time before
your people
started dying?
When all the letters could still be
sent,
all voices heard, embraces
exchanged,
every name
intact?

Now
it's like an old
cartoon,
with names dropping out
like teeth.

But
just like losing teeth,
no one
can ever tell you
how you'll
feel
about
the spaces.

Stained Glass

We sat there
guilty
to be alive when he was not.
Witnessing
the tragedies
beginning to unfold around him
helpless as he was
to prevent them.

I was poor then
went to his funeral in sapphire blue
because it was
the darkest dress I owned.
(I could never wear that dress much
after
though I tried
its colour always dazzled up my eyes
and took them
back to church.)

There was too much light in
that church.
Even
the stained-glass windows
should have known
how much of light
had gone away
with him.

We struggled
to offer comfort
but every word
only bore witness to the lightning bolt
the parents' loss
of everything
in their one
wonderful
boy.

The friend
his companion bookend
sunshine friendship
the envy of all.
They were inseparable
bright, laughing, teasing
searching
reaching
egging each other on
to pinnacles
gazing together in awe
beyond the borders
at places
their minds
had not yet gone.

Could we, should we
would even he
have prevented
the descent
precipitated by sorrow
and sudden loss
from glittering youth
to ordinary contentment?

Does death truly
take those
young
who are perfected early
nowhere to go
like roses
that open before noon
on hot summer days?

Or is death of roses
something
given to the rest of us
towards the acquisition
of wisdom?

From different angles...

December

Scre-e-crun-thud-d

Huddled around
Seven months growth
Of son,
You haul yourself out
Hollering,
"What-kind-of-a-left-turn-was-that?"

And she protests,
"It's not MY fault, lady,
He slammed me
Into your car!"

911
Red lights everywhere
Pulled over
Ambulance driver tells you
It's okay to keep crying.
Your
Husband's face
Through the car window
Through the snow,
Helping you into the ambulance.

You both get in
The other woman
And you.

And you hear the guy who hit you
Just keep asking
And asking
When he can phone for
A tow.

Diana

is
a clever contradiction
curls
and a hard hat

a warm wind
from the south
blowing laughter

secretly steel
stern, stoic
private

Empty Rooms

are
full of possibilities.

They say
you can't sell a house
empty
but I think you always
could
sell an empty house
to me.

Empty rooms
are
vital, on the brink

Like those decorating ads
where you see rooms
flash
through
innumerable
transformations
becoming
nurseries, dining rooms, dens,
studies, sitting rooms
"family" rooms
(when did they stop all being family rooms?)
in
rainbows of colours
oceans of fabric
warehouses of furniture

Yawning spaces
pristine and poised
in their stillness
to hold your future.

Old rooms
whispering silently
in other voices.

New rooms
breathlessly attending
voices
yet to be heard...
waiting

In time
we all walk through empty rooms
filling them.

The Floors

in my dreams are always
black and white.

Tiled chessboards
gleaming to infinity
in ballrooms
or foyers lit by chandeliers
or tucked away
in secret
paneled rooms.

They tilt and turn
zoomorphic;
sometimes they stretch
like cats
or shake themselves
like dogs.

You can't trust them;
you take a step
and suddenly find
they're mist
insubstantial
just reflections
of floors
somewhere in some mind;
you fall through them
or catch yourself
just in time
as you sink
up to the knee.

What messages are secreted
in those
perfectly sequenced squares of
black and white?

How do you read a recurring floor?

Forsythia

Whoever would have thought
forsythia
could be boring?

Golden showers and waterspouts
descending
like shouts
of yellow laughter.

It didn't make itself
dull
but dull's
out there.

Stunted
pruned
cut to bits
its

flowers scattered.

This
arrogant humanity
contrives
through
cultivation.

L'entranger

I dreamt
I was
an alien
reading
a book about
myself

I cheated
skipped to the ending

Hysterical
desperate
inconsolable
I cried,
Why does it have to end
like all the rest
with
waving
as I shoot back
to the stars?

Trees

There appear to be
two schools
of thought
about
trees.

One school
loves
to cut them down
clear things out
"brighten things up"
tidily
impose order.

The other school
loves shadows
finds them
dense and magical
lets the trees
go wild
irritating
those others.

Hard to say
(environmental issues aside)
whether it's worth
looking
for a compromise
any more than
you can ask
people
to change
their faces.

You Can't Write

good poems when
you're happy
she told me
and she should know
so I guess
all my poems are as bad
as this one
or
all this time
I've really been
miserable

Growing up Canadian...

About Winter

Sooner
or
later
Canadians
all write about
winter.

It's just
us.

Scents of Summer

Waves and whispers
of heat
float from sand
water
parked cars

On the beach
warmed by laughter
soothed by water
they lie
oiled seals
too close for comfort

Scents of metal
hints of mint
vague nuances of vanilla
slide over them
like shields
clouds
cover them
with summer

Summer in Saskatchewan

smelled
of heat, dust, caragana hedges,
and hot, dry flowers
sweet peas, Sweet William, bachelor's buttons, carnations
and lilac blooms left over from spring
that hadn't lost their fragrance
before the unrelenting sun
baked them on the branch

of sweat and gas cans for lawnmowers
lugged by dads and granddads
out of cool, dirt-floor
garages

of me and my brother
playing hide and seek with the neighbour kids
crouching in cubbies in the lilac trees
or the cool garages.

I see ya!
Quick jolt of surprise
and then a race through the shadows
home.

Swords, Knives and Daggers

are the weapons
of
winter
formed
by the slow
drip drip
of tears
from
the eavestroughs

Having a dog...

Dogs

When I had a dog
I wore youth
As an ill-fitting garment.
Clumsy,
I was always bumping into life.
Scratching myself
On its jagged edges,
Perpetually astonished
To watch
Crimson drops
As they disappeared
Into dust.

He was
Grace itself,
Whirling loose
From his collar,
Cutting through sunlight,
Turning
On a dime.
Accomplished,
He'd dive after ducks
In bright water.
When they bobbed up
Like corks,
He'd laugh.

People live longer
Than dogs.

Balker and the Babe

While everyone learned grief
the day that Balker's
cancer killed him,
he figured
the rest out as well:

"People are born to learn
to be good and love everyone,
right?"
he asked, rhetorically.
"Well, dogs know that already
so I guess that's why
they don't have to stay
as long."

Not bad for
four years old.

Only Human…

Antiques

Blue Willow pattern service
(a few pieces missing)
grit rolls under my fingers
as I touch a plate;
there are
just one or two scratches

She must have
kept them for best
Best Birthdays, Christmases
everybody home
while she cooked love
and polished
that service

You can smell the dust;
silence is suffocating
and yet
this shop is crowded
with company
around this table
(probably the same period as the service)

Might as well be me as
anyone else
I tell myself
while they're boxing
just one of
her plates.

Bath Water

There's something
profound
about bath water.

We sink
into its
warm, womblike
embrace
eyes closed
as it laps
lovingly
around us.

Who'd take
a shower?

That rough
baptism
wakes
and shakes us
into
consciousness.

In a bath
we become
aware
of our
primordial nature,
born to water.

(Bath births
are becoming
increasingly popular
I believe).

But bathers
must have
their masochistic side.

Why else would we
daily
inflict on ourselves
the pain
of pulling the plug
and watching
the water
cyclonically
swirl
out?

Getting Colours Done

There's a white
for everyone
she said
reassuringly

By which
I assume
there's a black
for
everyone
too

Guilt

is
a gash on your soul
that never stops
bleeding

Not to say
there's no
sunlight

Sometimes
in the distance
you can even hear
your own laughter

Then
the blood slows
to a trickle
drip
drip
behind the music

But in the dark
night
there's the
torment
gripping your gut
pulsing through
your veins
haunting
your dreams.

Martha

Since she got rich on
domesticity,
we'll all have
a lot of fun
if
there's an afterlife
watching her
trying to thread a needle
with a camel

Photograph

Flaxen-haired three-year-old
laughs behind
a birthday cake.

What are years
anyway
that one glance
can transport me
through so many of them
behind her eyes
to laugh behind
that cake?

Procrastination

    certainly
    makes life
    exciting.
Gnawing guilt, sense of dread
as the-thing-yet-to-be-done
  whispers somewhere:
You 'll never get me done...
    I'll tell

  It wakes you up
    at night,
  feeds your dreams
    with fear
 follows you through
    the day
    jeering.

Then,
seductively,
it leaves you to the
blotters out
giggling.
Go ahead...
there's always time
later...

One thing
it never does
though
is
the work.

You Know,

    she's a marvelous
        person

generous, observant, wise,
  an answer for every
      question

     I just think
   I could like her
       more

  If she were wrong
  more gracefully
      and
   more often

Things that go bump
in the night...

Ghost

That summer
When Harriet decided
To move into
The Old Blacksmith's House
She didn't realize
She'd be
Sharing it.

Night
After disturbed
Night
Unaccountably,
Came crashings
From the empty room
Below;
Everyone entering
That room
Even in hot summer daylight,
Felt the temperature
Drop.

Finally,
Harriet learned
How the prior occupant,
A woman
Grown elderly
Alone,
Moved her world
Into the
Cloistered shelter of
Her room
Seeking

Sanctuary?

She must have
Done it slowly,
Gradually,
Stick by stick,
Pulling the pieces of her life around her
Into Her Room
Wrapping herself in them
For protection,
Until, unconsciously,
She faded into the furniture.

What an appalling invasion
It must have been
To feel other souls around her,
Stamping through Her Room;
No wonder
She tried to freeze them out
And threw things
To frighten them
Away.

But it seems that she must have kept
Her manners,
Because, when Harriet,
Politely,
At four in the morning
Sat in the occupied emptiness
Of Her Room
And asked her if they couldn't
Live together,
She assented.

Perhaps, all those years,

She just wanted
Acknowledgement.

The House on Elm Tree Lane

Those of us who knew it best
were sure
it wasn't the house's fault.
It had gotten
a bad rep,
buried as it was
in cobwebs,
willows,
and wisteria,
lost
at the bottom
of
Elm Tree Lane.

All those nights
when we'd whispered
past it
on the way home
or
dared each other
to
clamber,
trembling,
up the crumbling
steps
to stand
for a heartbeat,
staring
at its cracked, black
glass,
the shuttered eyes
that should have been windows,
lifeless on that ragged
porch,
it had become
a part of our experience,
familiar in its daunting
strangeness:
The House on Elm Tree Lane,
we knew the directions.

Even though
that night
Emily,
with one last
glimmering
smile
at us
over her shoulder,
went in
and didn't come
out,
we're still sure
the house
didn't mean
to do
it.

Perhaps
it was just
lonely.

Stalker

He's at it
again.

Lurking in purple
shadows,
feeding
on her face,
swollen
with the power
of the coward
who can exact
his pound of terror,
lying
out of reach,
a disembodied
voice
out of the dark, his eyes
greedily feasting
on her frozen look
as she hears the
phone
ring.

Evil
doesn't have to be
grand scale;
Mephistopheles
Beelzebub
both live in minds
corroding
little corners
eating away at them
teasing, luring
"just once"
"just one more time"

And there
he is.

Women, men, and sometimes, love...

After Dark

Women walk differently after dark;
have you
noticed?

Women with men
sway slightly from the hips
shoulders soft,
leaning a little.

Women with women
lean on each other;
teens
giggle
as they grip each other,
swagger and stagger
hysterically.

Women with dogs
are also relaxed,
at ease;
they let the dogs
lead.

Women alone
stride tensely,
eyes front,
shoulders tight,
every atom broadcasting
"places to go"
fast.

The First Moment of Love

is
the hook
isn't it?
Full of fairytales, it's
a glimpse
into Ali Baba's cave.
Jewel light dancing in his eyes,
your prince glances up
to catch your entrance
as Cinderella,
dazzling.

There you are.
You take a step,
look down,
and see your toes curled
over the edge of
the precipice
you never suspected
was there.
The elevator suddenly
drops.

And then, the second
moment comes,
When you hear an ancient
goddess laughing
while the clock strikes
midnight,
and you wonder
what the hell you've
gotten yourself into
now.

Growing Fonder

Whoever said that absence
makes the heart grow fonder
should have his head examined
or examine it himself
(no woman ever dreamed up that remark)

What can it do but build up
distance
like a wall
dividing
minds and hearts

Intimacy
is an everyday thing
a messy thing
of arguments over nail clippings
in the sink
in-jokes must be
established
hands must be held
before hearts can
contract or expand
with someone else's
pain or joy

So you don't notice the other's
there
most of the time
no romantic visions
will be crushed
by their returning
presence
or require
bewildered, agitated
revision
at two in the morning
when you turn over
to find to your surprise
a foreign body
in your bed

When He Looked at Me

the other day
with such profound
distrust,
even though, thank God,
I'm a modem woman,
I thought
I smelled
burning.

Without You

it would be as though
my decapitated head
sat alone
on an island of granite
still able
to feel
agonizing pain
in my heart
suffering the hunger
of my lost body
howling its grief forever
to the four winds

Watching You

is like
standing beside
the tiger's cage
wondering
what would happen
if you put your hand
through
the bars.

Women and Men

touch you
differently.

Women
slide under your skin
dexterously
knowing just the right
words
to hurt
or heal.

Men
work from the outside
on
appearances
understanding
appears to be a matter
of interpreting
inferences.

But
it's the men
in your life
who
bare fisted
reach inside
to ache your heart
especially
when they try to make you
happy.

Acknowledgements

Grateful thanks to all the many people whose effort and encouragement made this collection possible: the production team at FriesenPress, especially Samuel, who oversaw so much of the process with me; Paul S., who so generously gave his time and talent to the design of the book and the creation of the cover, and to all of you who so kindly allowed me to force a reading on you, and whose responses gifted me with the impetus to continue with this project, especially Marilyn, Margaret, Pauline, Anne, Athena, JoAnn, Christopher, Amanda, Sherry, Paul F., and my gang of four—Lisa, Basia, Seth and Diana; to those who lent me a jump start at the beginning—Kim, Ellen, Nadia, Derek, Ryan and Angie, and to all of you who motivated me to push through to the end.

Finally, love and deepest thanks to Will, who inspired so many of these poems, and gave so much of his energy to the production of this collection, and to Lorne, who supported me through every page of it.

Printed in Canada